**soho
theatre
company**

by **Lin Coghlan**

Waking

**LONDON
ARTS BOARD**

Soho Theatre Company...

...at the Soho Poly

In 1972 Verity Bargate and Fred Proud established the Soho Theatre Company at the 50 seat Soho Poly. The mission was to produce new plays and discover new playwrights and the Company was to become a pioneering force in British Theatre.

Throughout the 70's and 80's the early work of such writers as Caryl Churchill, David Edgar, Hanif Kureishi, Tony Marchant, Sue Townsend and Timberlake Wertenbaker was premiered until the theatre – never an ideal performing space — was finally closed in 1990.

'If there is going to be any theatre apart from musicals in twenty years time, the Soho Theatre Company will probably have been its seed bed.'
The Tatler

Soho Theatre

...at the Cockpit

Under the new Artistic Direction of Abigail Morris, Soho Theatre Company relaunched in 1992 at the Cockpit Theatre. In three years there the Company presented more than 35 new plays and, in the words of the Ham and High created **'one of the leading centres for new writing in the country'**.

Plays premiered at the Cockpit included Karen Hope's *Ripped*; John Constable's *Tulip Futures*; Jonathan Lewis' *Our Boys*, Daniel Magee's *Paddywack* and Diane Samuels' *Kindertransport*.

soho
theatre
company

WAKING

LIN COGHLAN

N
H
B

...at 21 Dean Street

In July 1996 Soho Theatre Company took possession of the spectacular premises that will become our new and permanent home – **21 Dean Street**. In successfully acquiring the £3.1 million freehold, we became the first arts organisation to purchase a property on the open market with National Lottery funding.

With the building secure, Soho Theatre Company are entering the second phase of the project – the conversion of the building into the **Soho Theatre and Writers' Centre**. Scheduled to open in 1999 it will include an intimate theatre space, comprehensive backstage and rehearsal facilities, a Writers' Centre to house our pioneering development work with new writers and a lively bar/cafe. Designed by award-winning architects Paxton Locher, the new building will become a unique theatre where you can see the first works of a new generation of writers, right in the heart of the West End.

But before we let the builders in, we wanted to give a sneak preview. Lin Coghlan's **Waking** is part of **Site Specific**, a season of four new plays and a Writers' Showcase running until July 1997. We hope you enjoy the season and look forward to welcoming you back to 21 Dean Street in the future.

Soho Theatre Company will continue to produce elsewhere throughout the construction period. If you would like to be kept up to date, please call us on **0171 287 5060** to join our **free** mailing list.

Soho Theatre Company – a Writers' Theatre

Soho Theatre Company is a writers' theatre. Not only are we committed as a matter of policy to the production of new plays exclusively, but the company actively encourages new and emerging writers through its training and development programme. Central to our philosophy is the belief that playwriting – like any other craft – must be practiced to develop. We provide:

A script service reading and reporting on over 1500 scripts every year

A comprehensive writers' workshop programme

Rehearsed play readings

Script surgeries – *one to one dramaturgical support*

Writers' showcase productions

The Verity Bargate Award – *a biennial playwriting competition*

A bold commissioning policy

Send a play into our script reading service
At no cost to the writer, our readers' panel of theatre professionals will read, assess and advise on any play sent to us. Based on this assessment a decision will be made whether to consider the play further and how we might be able to help the writer develop their script.

The Workshop Programme
Writers showing promise may be invited to attend one of our various workshops. These range from skills workshops designed to heighten the participants' awareness of stagecraft, to those designed to examine in detail the writers' work-in-progress.

To find out
more please call
us on
0171 287 5060

Writer's note

Waking began life as a shorter play touring schools in East London, and was commissioned by The Half Moon Young Peoples Theatre. I had been working in Young Peoples' Theatre andTheatre in Education since leaving drama school, but I had not yet had the opportunity to write a story set completely in my native Ireland, and I owe a very great debt to The Half Moon YPT for making it possible. I would particularly like to take this opportunity to thank David Belshaw, who developed and directed the schools production, for his encouragement and faith in the play. It would not have been written without him. Subsequently the play was toured in youth clubs by Red Ladder.

Of necessity schools' productions must be short in order to fit in with the needs of the timetable, and I very much wanted to do further work on **Waking**, developing elements of the story in greater depth, and turning it into a full length play. I was delighted when Soho Theatre Company commissioned me to do just this.

I would particularly like to thank Abigail Morris and Paul Sirett for all their good advice during the re-writing process, Steve Keay and Steve Whiteman for letting **Waking** live with them in their house, and my friends John Dower and Deborah Bestwick for all their support and encouragement.

Lin Coghlan

Soho Theatre would like to thank the following
Monumental Masonry supplied by
Francis Chappell
Stone supplied by The Natural Stone Company
Sculptures, materials and tools courtesy of
Tony James
Statues supplied by Francis Chappell,
Frederica Banks and the Catholic Stage Guild
Hurley Sticks and Ball courtesy of
Mr and Mrs Dalton at the GA Club, Ruislip
Guinness courtesy of The Toucan Bar,
Carlisle Street, London W1
Crutches courtesy of Great Ormond Street
Hospital
Walking stick courtesy Age Concern,
Southwark
Consumables courtesy of J Sainsbury Plc

Special thanks to
Frances and Rev David Clayden at
Emmanuel Church
Susan Morrison and the City and Guilds of
London Art School
Terry Chappell at Carlton Home Entertainment
Valerie Cody and the Guinness Ireland Group
Royal Court Theatre
Tetrus Sounds
David Evans
Kevin McKeon
Crispin Dexter
Vivienne Enticott

Soho Theatre Company presents

Waking

by **Lin Coghlan**

Cast
in order of appearance

Sean Foley	**James Greene**
Michael Foley	**Steve Nicolson**
Brian Foley	**Lee Turnbull**
Sarah Burke	**Nicola Redmond**

*The story takes place
during a heat wave
one summer somewhere
on the Atlantic
Coast of Ireland*

Director	Abigail Morris
Designer	Tom Piper
Lighting Designer	Jason Taylor
Composer/Musician	Rebecca Rainsford
Sound equipment	Tetrus Sounds
Assistant Director	Carey Andrews
Assistant Director	Anna Coombs

Marketing and graphic design	Hardsell 0171 403 4037
Press representation	Bridget Thornborrow Arts Publicity 0171 379 3797
Casting	Marcia Gresham
Publicity photographs	Stuart Colwill

Production team

Production Manager	Julian Cree
DSM	Nicole Woodwood
ASM	Christopher Enticott
Box Office	First Call

*First perfomed on 6 March 1997 at Soho Theatre
Company's new premises at 21 Dean Street*

Lin Coghlan

Lin Coghlan is from Dublin. She trained at The Rose Bruford College on the no longer existing Community Theatre Arts Course.

After five years as an actor and director, she wrote her first play for Theatre Centre, *Fantastic Forgotten Voyage*. Since then she has written more than a dozen plays for young people in schools, youth clubs and community centres, including, *A Feeling in my Bones* and *Bretevski Street* also for Theatre Centre (both directed by Philip Osment), *Though the Heavens Fall* and *The Bus Shelter Show* for Red Ladder (both directed by Rachel Feldberg) and spending a year as resident writer under the Arts Council Resident Dramatist Award with The Half Moon Young Peoples Theatre, where she went on to write four plays, including the schools' version of *Waking* and *At the Edge of the Sky* (both directed by David Belshaw).

In 1996 she shared the Thames Television Theatre Writers Award and became writer in residence with The Soho Theatre Company, and later that year she wrote *The Night Garden* for the National Theatre Studio.

She is currently writing new plays for The Soho Theatre Company, and Teatrul Dramatic in Constanta, Romania.

Published work:
A Feeling in My Bones Thomas Nelson
Waking Nick Hern Books

James Greene *Sean*

Over the years James has worked with the National Theatre, Bristol Old Vic, Birmingham Rep, The Crucible Theatre and with BBC Radio Drama Company. Other theatre credits include *The Silver Tassie* and *Playboy of the Western World* at the Almeida (director Lynne Parker), *Pictures of Tomorrow* at the Lyric Theatre, Belfast (director Andy Hines) and *Una Pooka* at the Tricycle (director Nick Kent). Television credits include *Kavanagh QC* (Carlton UK), *Mapp and Lucia* (LWT) *Adam Bede* (BBC TV) and *Paradise Club* (Zenith/BBC TV). Film includes *Tom and Viv* (New Era Entertainments 1994) and *Empire of the Sun* (Warner Brothers 1987).

Abigail Morris *Director*

Abigail became Soho Theatre Company's Artistic Director in February 1992 and has since directed *Tulip Futures, The Rock Station* and *Kindertransport* (at the Cockpit, Watford and the Vaudeville) for them. She also directed *Kindertransport* with an American cast at the Manhattan Theatre Club, New York.

Additional credits include founder and director of Trouble and Strife Theatre Company for whom she adapted and directed *Present Continuous* (Fringe First Winner), wrote and directed *Queer Sultry Summer* and co-wrote and directed *Now and at the Hour of our Death* (Time Out and 01 for London Award) and *Next To You I Lie*.

Abigail has also directed Britten's *Noye's Fludde* (BBC Proms); Malcom Williamson's *Julius Caesar Jones* (Sadlers Wells); *Girls Who Score* (Minerva, Chichester); the British premiere of Cole Porter's *Leave it To Me* (Arts, Cambridge) and Cleo Lane and Jackie Dankworth in *Suitcase Four*.

Steve Nicolson *Michael*
Theatre credits include *Dealers Choice*, National Theatre Tour (director Patrick Marber); *Blue Remembered Hills* at the Crucible (director Deborah Warner): *What I Did in the Holidays* (director Mike Alfreds) and *A Taste of Honey*, English Touring Theatre (director Polly Teale). Television credits include *Bergerac* (BBC TV) ; *Casualty* (BBC TV); *Between the Lines* (BBC TV); *Dangerfield* (BBC TV) *Comics* (CH4); *A Touch of Frost* (YTV); *Martin Chuzzlewit* (BBC TV), playing the part of Mark Tupley, and the forthcoming *The Investigator* (CH4). Film includes *Let Him Have It* and *All Men are Mortal*.

Tom Piper *Designer*
Tom graduated from Trinity College, Cambridge in 1988 before attending the Slade School of Art to train in theatre design. Tom's design work includes *Six Characters in Search of an Author* and *The Crucible* (The Abbey, Dublin); *Sweet Panic* and *The Philanderer* (Hampstead); *Endgame*, *Dumbstruck, Macbeth, Cinderella* and *Jack and the Beanstalk* (Tron, Glasgow); *Much Ado About Nothing*,

A Patriot to Me; Spring Awakening and *The Broken Heart* (Royal Shakespeare Company); *The Duchess of Malfi* (Greenwich and West End); *Blinded by the Sun, The Birthday Party* (Royal National Theatre); *Tulip Futures, My Goat, Ripped, Kindertransport* and *The Rock Station* – for which he received the London Fringe Award for Best Design 1992/3 (Soho Theatre Company); *Sacred Hearts* (Communicado); *The Master Builder* (Royal Lyceum, Edinburgh); *The Price* (York, Theatre Royal); *The Way Of The World* (Lyric, Hammersmith); *The Masked Ball* (Dublin Grand Opera); *The Cherry Orchard* (Nottingham Playhouse); *Golem* (Northern Stage Company and Northern Sinfonia); *The Dark River, Cat With Green Violin, His Majesty, Mrs Warren's Profession* and *We, The Undersigned* (Orange Tree); *No-one Writes to the Colonel* (Lyric Studio, Hammersmith); *La Churga* and *The Healer* (The Old Red Lion); *A Cat in the Ghetto* – for which he received the London Fringe Award for Best Design 1989/90 – (Tabard, Chiswick) and *Noye's Fludde* (St James Church, Piccadilly and The Royal Albert Hall). Future productions include *Spanish Tragedy* (Royal Shakespeare Company); *Wallace and Gromit – A Grand Night Out; Backpay* and *Cockroach, Who?* (Royal Court, Young Writers' Festival).

Rebecca Rainsford *Composer/Musician*
Rebecca trained at Rose Bruford College where she specialised as an actor/musician. Theatre credits include Gretel in *Hansel and Gretel* (Northumberland Theatre Company); May in Brian Friels' *Lovers* (Vienna English Theatre); Princess Dahlia in *Aladdin* (London Bubble);*Caucasian Chalk Circle* and *The Lost Child* (Royal Theatre Northampton); Josephine Sleary and lead musician in *Hard Times* (The Good Company).

She is also a trained singer and has written and performed music for several plays including *Much Ado About Nothing, Macbeth* and *Romeo and Juliet.*

Nicola Redmond *Sarah*
Theatre credits include *The Duchess of Malfi*, Cheek by Jowl (director Declan Donnellan); *Bearing Fruit*, Hampstead Theatre (director Deborah Paige); *Phoenix; The Baby* ,The Bush Theatre (directors Dominic Dromgoole, Polly Irvin); *Children of the Dust, Me and My Friend*, Soho Theatre Company (directors Terry Johnson, Deborah Paige); *Ragdoll*, Bristol Old Vic (director Terry Johnson); *Three Sisters*, Wolsey (director Hettie MacDonald); *Death and the King's Horsemen*, Royal Exchange (director Phyllida Lloyd); *The Good Sisters*, Sheffield Crucible (director Mark Brickman); *Macbeth, Trewlawney of The Wells, Beaux Stratagem* at the Royal National (directors Richard Eyre, John Caird

and Peter Wood). Nicola is currently in the new series of *Silent Witness* (BBC TV). Other TV credits include *Goodnight Sweetheart* (Alamo Productions for BBC TV); *Pie in the Sky* (Select TV); *Boy Soldier*(CH4); Ruth Rendell's *The Secret House of Death* (Blue Heaven Productions); *Capital Sins* (CH4); *Three Seven Eleven* (Granada TV) and In *Suspicious Circumstances* (Granada TV).

Jason Taylor *Lighting Designer*
Jason trained at the Royal Exchange Theatre, Manchester, before moving to Nottingham Playhouse as Head of Lighting, where productions included *Godspell, A Midsummer Nights Dream, Prisoners, Salad Days, An Enemy of The People* and five pantomimes and thirty other productions. Regional credits include *Oliver* (York Theatre Royal); *You Never Can Tell* (West Yorkshire Playhouse); *The Seagull* (Orange Tree, Richmond); *Romeo and Juliet* (Scarborough); *Tulip Futures* (Soho Theatre Company); *The Office Party* (Watford); *The Glass Menagerie, The Woman Who Cooked Her Husband, Oleanna, Burn This* and *The Dresser* (Theatre Royal, Plymouth); *Misery, For Services Rendered, Just Between Ourselves, A Going Concern* and *Forty Years On* (Scarborough); *A View From The Bridge* (York, Theatre Royal); *Office Suite* (West Yorkshire Playhouse); *Hay Fever* (Crucible, Sheffield); *The Dark Side* (Bill Kenwright Ltd). London credits include six seasons at Open Air

Theatre, Regents Park, including *A Midsummer Night's Dream, Hamlet, Macbeth, The Card, A Connecticut Yankee, Richard III* and *The Music Man; And Then There Were None* (Duke of Yorks); *Rosencrantz and Guildenstern are Dead (Piccadilly); Kindertransport* (Vaudeville). National tours include *On the Piste; Bedroom Farce; The Hobbit; Feed; Last Tango In Whitby; Erik The Viking; Fallen Angels; Dancing at Lughnasa*. International work includes *Sweet Sorrow* (Los Angeles); *The Taming Of The Shrew* (Middle East tour); *Blood Brothers* (New Zealand/Australia tour). Non theatre includes interior lighting design for The Emaginator – a virtual reality cinema at the Trocedero, London; Lighting Consultant for Soho Theatre Company's new theatre.

Lee Turnbull *Brian*
Theatre credits include *1953* at the Almeida and *Liberation of Skopje*, for Moving Theatre. Television includes *Eastenders* (BBC TV); *Famous Five* (BBC TV); *The Vet* (Ikona Films); *The Bill* (Thames); *No Bananas* (BBC) and *The Childrens Society* (ITV). Film credits include *Clockwork Mice* (Metrodome) and *Willie's War* (Childrens Film Unit). Radio credits include *Mirad-boy from Bosnia* (BBC World Service).

WAKING

For Philip

whose craftsmanship has been such an inspiration to me

'Waking' could not have been written without the help of a number of friends and colleagues. I would particularly like to thank David Belshaw who listened to the story at every stage, John Dower whose strength and enthusiasm propelled me through many a dark moment in the process, Deborah Bestwick for everything. Steve Keay and Steve Whiteman for living with it in the same house, and my friend and colleague Philip Osment whose craftsmanship has been such a source of inspiration to me.

Lin Coghlan

Cast

SEAN FOLEY	60's Southern Irish
MICHAEL FOLEY	30's Sean's son, has acquired an English accent.
BRIAN FOLEY	13, Michael's son, born in England.
SARAH BURKE	30's, Sean's next door neighbour.

The story takes place during a heat wave, one summer, somewhere on the Atlantic Coast of Ireland.

ACT ONE

Scene One

The set is the yard of Sean Foley's masonry business, somewhere on the Atlantic coast of Ireland.

To the right is Sean's house, off.

To the left, a crumbling Sea Wall, sandy in colour, a few flowers somehow are managing to grow between the cracks.

The yard is piled high with old plaster holy statues, gravestones and the bits and pieces of the trade.

It is very hot.

Sean is working away in the yard. He stops, and looks as if he might be expecting someone. He goes back to work. He stops again, and after a moment exits.

Michael enters on crutches. He looks around the yard.

Brian enters. He is carrying two heavy cases.

Sean enters and sees Michael. The two men look at each other, neither moves, the gap doesn't close between them.

SEAN   You're here then.

MICHAEL   Yeah. The plane was late.

SEAN   Was it?

Neither man makes a move.

SEAN   I was working.

MICHAEL   We'll get unpacked then.

SEAN   Right you are.

Sean goes back to work.

Michael and Brian exit with their cases.

Music.

Scene Two

The next day.

Sean is working away at a stone, lettering a gravestone.

Brian is on the Sea Wall with his headphones on.

Michael enters on crutches, his left foot bare. He carries his shoe and sock in one hand.

MICHAEL   Dad? The milkman wants his money.

SEAN   Tell him we'll pay him next week.

MICHAEL   He's hovering at the door.

Sean gets up and wipes his hands.

SEAN   What does he think we'll do, make a run for it?

Sean exits to the house.

Michael hands Brian his shoe and sock, and Brian puts them on for him.

Sean comes back.

SEAN   That bit of garden out the front is like a desert in this heat.

Sean wipes his neck in the heat.

SEAN   That boy could do a bit of lettering, couldn't he, instead of sitting around bored.

MICHAEL   He doesn't want to.

SEAN   He can speak for himself, he's got a tongue in his head hasn't he? We didn't have these long holidays in the old days Brian, the boys always worked through the summer break, isn't that right? Sure you'd be bored out of your skull sitting around, wouldn't you? Your dad did the whole of the nuns' graveyard up at Carraroe one summer.

MICHAEL   It was a terrible job.

SEAN   And he was only your age.

MICHAEL   It was a terrible job.

SEAN   Work was never meant to be a joyride. Come on now Brian, let's see what you can do.

MICHAEL   He doesn't know one end of a chisel from the other.

SEAN   So he can learn.

4

MICHAEL	He doesn't want to learn.
SEAN	Listen to me Brian and I'll tell you something now. The thing with stone is that it's in your blood, do you understand that? The stone is in your blood and there's nothing you can do about it. Come on now boy.

Brian takes the chisel and hammer.

MICHAEL	Dad!
SEAN	Let the boy be Michael.

Brian taps out a bit of a letter.

SEAN	What did I tell you! Go into the kitchen Brian and bring out that big bottle of lemonade before we all die of thirst.

Brian exits.

Michael and Sean bake in the yard.

SEAN	Is you foot sore?
MICHAEL	It's alright.
SEAN	You could have lost a leg.

The silence hangs between them.

Brian enters with the lemonade.

SEAN	Good man

Sean drinks from the bottle, he offers it to Michael who refuses, then to Brian who drinks from it.

BRIAN	The butter's gone all melted on the plate.
SEAN	It's like an oven in the house.
MICHAEL	You should get a fridge. It's ridiculous not having a fridge in this day and age.
SEAN	Sure we've never needed a fridge in this house. What are we meant to be, the Shellbourne Hotel?
MICHAEL	He was too mean to buy Mam a fridge.
SEAN	What was that?

Pause. No one speaks.

SEAN	Are there any boats on the water today Brian?

Brian gets up on the Sea Wall.

BRIAN	There's a blue and yellow one.

5

SEAN	That'll be Deccy's boat. Is there a fella in it with a stupid hat on him?
BRIAN	Yeah, there is.
SEAN	Didn't I tell you?
BRIAN	What kind of hat is it?
SEAN	It's one of those bicycle hats from England.
MICHAEL	They have them over here too da.
SEAN	Well, I've never seen one and I'm up and down that road every day.
MICHAEL	You mean a helmet.
SEAN	Doesn't it take the biscuit?
BRIAN	Why's he wearing a cycling helmet in a boat?
SEAN	The divil knows, he's been out in the sun too long if you ask me.

Sean pauses again in the heat.

SEAN	There's no shade in this bloody yard.
MICHAEL	And no shelter.

Brian is looking at the plaster statues that are scattered around the yard.

SEAN	Watch out for those statues Brian, you look at them long enough and they start looking back at you.
BRIAN	Did you make them?
SEAN	No, no, no, we've never made statues here, sure I can't do a damn thing in the round, I can only see it flat on. Frontways on. If I try making it any other way it always comes out looking like an old horse. You see doing sticky out bits on a statue is murder. Why do you think the Blessed Virgin never has sticky out hands, answer me that? She always has them like this, or with a bunch of flowers or what have you. That's 'cause sticky out hands are murder. So now you know.
	Did Chris come and see you in the hospital Mike?
MICHAEL	No.
SEAN	Did she not come?
MICHAEL	I didn't want her to come.

6

Michael exits. Brian gets up on the sea wall.

Sean goes away.

> You like it up on that old bit of wall, don't you?
> Your dad was born into this house on a lovely
> summery day like this one, did you know that?
> In the big bedroom upstairs. And your Aunt
> Berni who's gone to Australia now, she was only
> three and I took her up to see the new baby and
> she made me come out here afterwards and leave
> bread on the wall for the stork in case it was
> hungry. For she thought the stork had brought
> the baby and it'd be tired. So we left bread on
> the wall for it.

Sean works. Pause.

> Why would anyone want to live in Australia?

BRIAN   Her boyfriend's a drummer. He has his nose
             pierced.

SEAN   He has what?

BRIAN   He has his nose pierced so he can put a stud in it.

SEAN   Yeah, well that's pop singers for you. Come
             over here to me. What do you see?

BRIAN   A rock.

SEAN   But is there good stone inside it?

BRIAN   I don't know.

SEAN   Yes you do. Feel it.

Brian puts his hand on the stone.

> Can you feel good stone inside it? Good cutting
> stone with no white horses running through it.

BRIAN   What's that?

SEAN   White horses? Like this. We don't want those.

Brian stands with his hands on the stone.

> Ah it'll come, Rome wasn't built in a day.

Michael comes out with a bottle of Guinness in his hand.

MICHAEL   What's going on?

SEAN   We're throwing in the rag, aren't we Brian?

MICHAEL   I don't see why you're working at all, you can't
             make any money out of this stuff.

SEAN	Working's good for the soul.

Sean and Michael stare uneasily at each other.

Pause.

SEAN	We don't all have your compensation money in the bank. Your dad's rolling in it.
MICHAEL	Do you want some?
SEAN	Of course I do not.
MICHAEL	You wouldn't take it anyway.
SEAN	You're damn right I wouldn't. I've never taken a handout in my life.
MICHAEL	And I have?
SEAN	(to Brian) Jesus, how can you wear all those clothes in this heat? How can the boy wear all those clothes? You'll be bursting into flames any minute. Would you not take that jacket off?

Brian doesn't. Sean climbs up on the sea wall.

	The little sailing boats are coming out of the harbour now. There must be a lovely cool breeze out over the water.
MICHAEL	Brian, will you take that walkman out of your ears.
SEAN	To have a sailing boat must be grand. Your dad won medals racing little yachts for the Navy, did you know that Brian?
MICHAEL	The Portsmouth team, not the Navy.
SEAN	What possessed him to join the Navy now I couldn't tell you, it's always been a mystery to me.
MICHAEL	Brian!

Brian takes his headphones off.

	Do you have to wear that thing all the time? Christ, aren't you able to talk?

All three stand in silence listening to the sea.

A bell rings.

Sean blesses himself.

SEAN	That'll be the Angelus now.

The bell continues ringing, the three men listening.

Sarah climbs up over the sea wall. In one hand she has two beautiful freshly caught silver fish, with the other she empties the sand out of her shoes.

SARAH	I have the fishes, now all we need is the loaves.
SEAN	How are ya Sarah?
SARAH	Grand.
SEAN	Those are a couple of fine beasts you're after catching.
SARAH	They're huge, aren't they? I nearly had the arms pulled out of me, I thought I must have caught a motor boat and not a fish at all. Hasn't it been a glorious day?
SEAN	Come down. This is Michael, and this is the grandson Brian.
SARAH	Hello, it's lovely seeing you both over. Will I put these in the kitchen Sean?
SEAN	Go on and do.

Sarah exits to the kitchen off.

MICHAEL	What's she doing here?
SEAN	She's come over for her tea.
MICHAEL	You mean she's eating with us?
SEAN	What's the matter with you?
MICHAEL	I don't want you asking people over just 'cause I'm here.
SEAN	Sarah always comes over on a Friday.
MICHAEL	It's very cosy, isn't it? This is the one next door who used to be a nun.
SEAN	She isn't a nun anymore.
MICHAEL	Do you hear that Brian, she used to be a nun.

Sarah has come out and overheard the last line.

SARAH	God Sean, you're after killing that clematis in the space of a week.
SEAN	I did nothing to it at all.
SARAH	I can well believe it, when did you last give it a drop of water?
SEAN	I can't remember to do everything.
SARAH	How are you feeling Michael? Your dad told me about the accident, is your leg better now?

MICHAEL	It's great, that's why I'm walking around on these crutches.
SEAN	Shut your mouth you, I won't have that kind of talk in this house.

Pause.

SARAH	I should go and clean the fish.
SEAN	Do you know where the sharp knife is?

Sean follows Sarah off.

MICHAEL	We don't have to stay here you know. We can go home any time you like.
BRIAN	It's alright. It's better than Portsmouth.
MICHAEL	Oh right, I get it, anything's better than being stuck on your own with me for the holiday.
BRIAN	Mum gave me a message for you.
MICHAEL	Did she? Well I don't want to hear it.

Sean enters.

SEAN	Red lemonade. You don't have red lemonade in England do you? I asked for it in a pub once and they thought I was mad. God, it'd be a great night for a swim. Do you want to go in for a swim, Brian?
MICHAEL	No he doesn't want to go for a swim. He's afraid of the water.
SEAN	That's stupid. I taught all me children to swim.
MICHAEL	He use to throw us in, didn't you dad?
SEAN	It never did you any harm. Come on and we'll all sit down and have a jar.
MICHAEL	You're not giving him a drink.
SEAN	Did I say I was going to give the boy a drink?

Sarah comes out drying her hands on a tea towel.

SARAH	You'll never guess what I saw today Sean.
SEAN	Go on, tell me.
SARAH	Rory McNamara in a canoe.
SEAN	No!
SARAH	As God is my judge. I don't know how he ever got into it, he must be ninety if he's a day.

SEAN	A canoe?
SARAH	I'm telling you, a lime green canoe.
SEAN	Good for him, maybe it's white water rafting he's going in for.
BRIAN	I've seen that on the telly.
SEAN	Did you do canoeing in the Navy, Mike?
MICHAEL	Yes, we did canoeing.
SEAN	You could have a lend of Rory's canoe.
MICHAEL	I don't want a lend of Rory's canoe
SEAN	It'd be perfect, it's good exercise and you don't need your legs for it.
MICHAEL	Thanks. Thanks for working it all out.
SEAN	What have I said now? Honest to God Sarah, it's like walking on glass with him.

Sarah sits at the table.

SARAH	How long are you over for Michael?
MICHAEL	I don't know. Will I get the plates Dad?
SEAN	Will you sit down there for a single minute and talk.
MICHAEL	Brian! Brian! If you don't take those headphones out of your ears, I'm telling you, I'll smash that thing to bits, do you hear me?
SARAH	(TO SEAN) Are you busy?
SEAN	Busy enough. Ah sure the recession never matters much in this trade, people don't stop dying.

Pause.

SARAH	Thank God for craftsmen, in no time at all they'll be sticking polystyrene stones over people's graves and running them up in a factory.
SEAN	You're not codding me, the business will die with me.
SARAH	And what are you up to Michael?
MICHAEL	Nothing.
SEAN	He was in the Navy, invalided out.
SARAH	That must have been a great life.
SEAN	He got compensation, God he did.

MICHAEL	I can talk for myself.
SEAN	I wish you would then, it's like trying to get blood out of a turnip.
SARAH	And is this your first time over Brian?
SEAN	They came over when he was a baby with his mother, Christine.
MICHAEL	We're separated.
SEAN	'Separated'. God Almighty. They're all like that in England.

Pause.

Chris was a real gas, I loved that girl.

Sarah goes up to the sea wall.

SARAH	It's still lovely and warm.

Sarah looks out to sea.

Come here Brian, come here and look, look, there's a seal out there and it has a fish in its mouth, do you see it? There.

Brian looks at the seal with Sarah.

SEAN	Oh we get seals out there in the deep water, oh God we do. Do you remember when Timmy Hagen used to keep that pet seal in his Granny's bath Mike? Do you? Jesus, the smell nearly destroyed the house. They had to get the fumigation lorry out from Athenry.
SARAH	There's a heat haze up over the city.
BRIAN	Where is it?
SARAH	Galway. That's Galway, and out there are the Aran Islands, Inishmore and Inishman, Inisheer, and then America, thousands of miles across the sea.
MICHAEL	I'll get the plates.
SEAN	What's the matter with him? Can he not sit still.

Pause.

Brian's twelve.

BRIAN	Thirteen
SEAN	Oh that's right, thirteen. When I was thirteen I was working in the yard.

SARAH	But that was back in the nineteenth century Sean.
SEAN	Go on out of that.
SARAH	Well listen to yourself. Brian doesn't want to hear your life story and neither do I.
SEAN	I'll leave you to it then and have a wash.

Sean exits.

SARAH	Well Brian, I'm delighted to meet you after all this time. You're famous here you know.
BRIAN	Am I?
SARAH	Oh yes. The only grandchild. It must be terribly quiet for you here though. There's not too much to do.
BRIAN	It's alright. (Pause) Do you know Berni?
SARAH	No, she's never been over.
BRIAN	She sings in a band.
SARAH	Thats right.
BRIAN	In Australia. Her bloke's the drummer.
SARAH	I know. What sort of stuff do they play?
BRIAN	Heavy Metal. It's loud, you wouldn't like it.
SARAH	I like Guns and Roses and they're heavy metal aren't they?
BRIAN	You like Guns and Roses?
SARAH	They came to Dublin. I went.

Michael comes out with the knives and forks. He looks at them, they look back at him, he leaves.

SARAH	And tell me, what's your Dad like normally?
BRIAN	How do you mean?
SARAH	I mean is he always like this? Like a bag of angry cats?
BRIAN	He got his legs caught under a lorry at work, on an exercise. He had to go to a special hospital. They said maybe he wouldn't be able to walk again, but he can now. He has steel pins in his leg right up to his hip.
SARAH	And did you go and see him in the hospital?
BRIAN	Yeah.

SARAH	That must have been hard for you, to see your Dad like that.
BRIAN	When he first woke up he couldn't feed himself. I fed him. Muesli. I put honey on it 'cause he doesn't really like muesli.

Michael comes out drinking a bottle of Guinness.

Sean follows.

SEAN	There's a nice smell from the kitchen.
SARAH	Is there now?

Sean sits down and peels some potatoes.

SARAH	And do you play any music yourself Brian?
BRIAN	Guitar.
SEAN	Do you remember when Timmy Hagen used to play the tin tray Mike, God it was murder.
MICHAEL	Am I having a vision or what?

Everyone looks at Michael as he drinks.

MICHAEL	I said am I having a vision or what? Is that my father peeling a potato?
SEAN	Come and sit down Michael, we haven't had a proper chat yet.
MICHAEL	You're trying to shut me up aren't you?
SEAN	You just watch your mouth.
SARAH	Come on Brian, help me water the plants.

They water the plants and end up near the wall.

SEAN	Are you drunk?
MICHAEL	I wish I was.
SEAN	I won't have you here and drunk.
MICHAEL	Throw me out then.

Michael goes to leave.

SEAN	Are you going so?
MICHAEL	I am. I'm going to the pub.
SEAN	Before your tea and Sarah's cooking it for you?

Michael goes.

SEAN	Well God blast you then.

Sean stands looking after Michael, furious.

Jesus, I could give him a good belt. What does he want eh? Tell me? Does he think the whole world circulates around him or what? Jesus Christ!

Scene Three

Three Hours Later.

Brian lies sleeping on top of the Sea Wall. Sarah and Sean sit at the table, the remains of the meal still surrounding them. Sean belts the radio to make it come on.

The radio plays.

Sarah is taking the stalks off some strawberries.

RADIO   Radio Telifis Eireanne, it's 9.00 o'clock, here is the shipping forecast . . .

Sarah dips a strawberry in the sugar and eats it.

SEAN   I thought you had those for the jam?

SARAH   I'm testing the batch.

Sean looks at Sarah.

SARAH   What?

SEAN   How many are you going to eat before the test is finished?

Sarah dips another strawberry in the sugar and hands it to Sean.

SARAH   You can be my assistant.

SEAN   Oh fair enough so.

SARAH   Look there's the first star out now.

Sean eats the strawberry.

Pause.

SEAN   They never came back, not one of them, unless it was to see their mother. Spread out now across the world so they are.

SARAH   Will you look at himself. Do you think he's asleep?

SEAN   When you're young you can sleep anywhere.

SARAH   Well now, isn't he yours and he's not at the far end of the world.

SEAN	Is he mine indeed?
SARAH	He's the spitting image of you.

Pause.

	Will you listen to the sea.

They listen.

SEAN	What am I listening for?
SARAH	Just the sound of the water coming up to the land. I love that sound.
SEAN	She's mad as a goat this one.
SARAH	To live by the sea is to live on the edge of a mystery, do you not think so?
SEAN	Mad as a goat.

A song comes on the radio. Sean sits smoking and listening looking out to sea.

RADIO	When youth was mine in health and prime I longed for wealth and fame An adventurous one of love controlled Of Wicklow rebel strain
SEAN	(Joining in absentmindedly)
	I wandered down to Edwardstown Unknown, unloved, unseen I met a girl, a matchless pearl My County Leitrim queen

Sarah turns the radio down and leaves Sean singing on his own.

	Her hair was like the sunkissed gold Her cheeks a lily hue No crayon chisel broach or pen Could express my colleen rua.
	The beauty she possessed was rare The affection n'er I've seen In the love that mirrored from her eyes My County Leitrim queen.
SARAH	Where did you learn all those songs?
SEAN	In pubs in Kilburn. You could make a fortune singing that old stuff on a Saturday night. Sure I never knew any songs atall until I went to England.
SEAN	What's that hammering?

Pause.

16

They must be putting the tents up in the long field for the fair tomorrow.

Sean looks at Brian as he lies on top of the wall.

SEAN	It's a long time since there's been a child in this house.
SARAH	Does he remind you of Michael, when he was that age?
SEAN	Mike? God I don't know.
SARAH	Do you not remember so? What he was like?
SEAN	I was working. We worked from dawn til dusk in the old days, that was real work. And in the summers I'd be on the buildings over in England, that was a great crack, those fellas were up for anything.
SARAH	But you'd be away?
SEAN	You went where the work was, and you sent the money home.

Michael arrives in the yard. He is drunk.

MICHAEL	I could find my way back on the road with my eyes shut.
SEAN	It's well for you.
MICHAEL	Brian! Brian! Do you know something? That road's just the same. In the moonlight, with the trees, it's just the same as when I was a child. Just the same.
SEAN	You've missed your tea.
SARAH	Leave it Sean.
MICHAEL	How many times did you miss your tea. Breakfast, dinner and tea?
SEAN	You're drunk.
MICHAEL	I'm not. I am not. Brian? Brian? When did you ever see me drunk before I had my accident?

Brian slips down over the other side of the wall and away.

MICHAEL	Brian?
SARAH	There's food left, would you eat something?
MICHAEL	I don't want anything.

17

SARAH	Oh I'm sure you could manage something.
MICHAEL	I said I don't want it. Did you not hear me. I don't want anything from you.

Sean takes Michael by the arm.

MICHAEL	Get off me.

Michael bumps into the table and upsets a jug of water over his injured foot.

SARAH	Let me help you.
MICHAEL	No I'm alright.
SEAN	You clumsy eegit, you're wet through.

Sean exits.

Sarah and Michael stand in silence.

Sean comes back in.

SEAN	I have dry socks for you.
MICHAEL	Leave me alone.
SEAN	I can put them on you.
MICHAEL	I don't want you to. I don't want you to.

Sean throws the socks down.

SEAN	Ah god blast you. Is it Lord Muck you think you are? God blast you.

Sean exits furious.

Michael stands, wet, miserable, staring ahead. Sarah gets a chair from the table and draws it forward for him.

SARAH	There's a chair for you now.

After a moment Michael sits. He lets his crutches slip down by his side. Sarah exits and then comes back with a towel. She looks at Michael but he cannot return her gaze. She kneels down beside him and she starts to take off his sock.

SARAH	There's a strange thing about these balmy summer evenings, do you not think so? The shock of the coolness after the heat of the day.

Sarah takes Michael's foot in her lap and dries it with a towel.

	You can hear all the sounds that normally you'd never notice atall, and the smell of people cooking sausages and blackpudding with their windows open.

Michael looks at Sarah as she continues drying his foot.

18

It's like the scent of that big bush down by the
back gate. That's a very old bush, isn't it? That
must have been there since you were a child. I
love the smell of the bush. When I come home at
night, I close my eyes so I can think of nothing
except the smell of that blossom before I go into
my bed.

Sarah finishes dressing Michael's foot. He cannot stop looking at
her.

Scene Four

The next afternoon.

Brian is looking out to sea plaiting some rope that has been washed
up on the beach. The sea comes and goes. The heat hangs like a
blanket over the yard. Brian's clothes have started to take on the
ghostly white of the dust from the stone.

Sen enters smoking, slipping his keys into his pocket and checking
his trousers for his wallet. He starts to set his watch, goes to the
radio gives it a good thump, which gets it going.

RADIO   And remember, if you want healthy sheep, use
                 McClenagans. McClenagans is the best sheep
                 dip.

SEAN   Ah will you shut up and give me the time for
                 God's sake.

BRIAN   Alright?

SEAN   Jesus! You frightened the life out of me. Do you
                 want me to have another heart attack?

BRIAN   Sorry.

SEAN   Do you know what the time is?

BRIAN   Nearly four.

Sean sets his watch.

SEAN   The days nearly over and not a child in the house
                 is washed.

Sean looks at Brian.

SEAN   Have you been stuck up on top of that wall like
                 an old gargoyle since your breakfast?

Pause.

> Listen, I have to do a gatepost for the Girl
> Guides and I haven't even got under way yet.
> You couldn't just chip an old owl out of that bit
> of rock could you? Sure you couldn't do worse
> than me, I haven't even seen an owl. (He shouts)
> Michael! MICHAEL!

Michael comes to the kitchen door on crutches, he carries his shoes
and a tin of shoe polish.

SEAN   It's four o'clock. Have you been up in your bed
                half the day?

Michael doesn't reply.

> Listen, I'm off into town. I have to go to the
> bank. Is there anything you want?

MICHAEL   No thanks.

SEAN   Will I see what's on at the pictures?

MICHAEL   If you want.

SEAN   What about the boy? What would he like to do?
                There's that Independence Day thing on, or
                maybe that was last week.

MICHAEL   Don't bother for me.

SEAN   I'll be back before tea then.

Sean goes. Michael sits down and starts to polish his shoes.

MICHAEL   You can't do spit and polish if you've eaten
                chicken, did you know that? It gets in the spit
                and breaks up the polish. Some of the lads used
                to cheat on inspection, spray their boots with
                ignition seal. You could always tell.

Michael holds out his left shoe to Brian and the boy helps him on
with it. Michael puts the other shoe on himself.

MICHAEL   What do you make of that woman from next
                door?

BRIAN   She's alright.

Michael goes to the rough exercise bar he's made and starts to do
pull ups.

> 1 ... 2 ... 3 ... 4 ...

> It's weird she was a nun. I mean you'd have to
> be a bit round the bend, wouldn't you? Here
> Brian, do you want to do some pull ups on the
> bar?

BRIAN	I'm no good at it.
MICHAEL	Course you are, I'll show you how.
BRIAN	It's alright.

Michael continues exercising.

MICHAEL	I used to be able to do 250 sit ups when I was on the team. Do you remember coming with your mum to watch us at Olympia?
BRIAN	I was sick on the tube coming home.
MICHAEL	Oh well fine, just as long as you remember being sick on the tube.

Michael continues exercising, finally coming to a stop.

He and Brian have nothing to say.

MICHAEL	I'll put the kettle on.

Michael exits. Brian looks at Sean's work, the engraving and interlacing. Sarah climbs up over the wall and shakes the sand out of her shoes.

SARAH	How are ya Brian?
BRIAN	Hello.
SARAH	The sun's above us and God's in his heaven. What are you up to today?
BRIAN	I don't know.

Sarah stares at Brian a long time. He begins to feel uncomfortable. They smile at each other.

SARAH	God you have the ears worn off me with all your chatting. Don't fall into that old trap Brian.
BRIAN	What trap?
SARAH	I'll tell you, and it's something I've learned after years of experience. Men aren't always altogether gifted in talking department. Sometimes you have to rush at them and hit them over the head with a conversation before you can get any joy out of them at all. Oh the noise they make would baffle you at times, but a conversation, it can be a struggle and no mistake. But you're not like that, are you Brian? I can see that. You have plenty to say, plenty.

Michael enters with two mugs in his hand.

MICHAEL	If you're looking for dad he's gone into town.

SARAH	Has he now? Do you know what I've discovered? Terry O'Donahue's moving picture lorry is coming into the village tonight and the film's *Rambo!* Can you imagine! I can't wait!
BRIAN	What is it?
SARAH	He has his father's old film projector strapped to the roof of the van . . .

Sarah waters the flowers as she explains.

	And he goes round the local villages in the summer, on the fine nights, showing the films onto the wall of any big white building he can find, and tonight it's us! He'll do it on the side of Nancy's bar over the river and if you stand on a table you can see it from here.
MICHAEL	What are you suggesting? That we all stand on a table in the yard just so we can see some daft old man projecting a pile of mindless rubbish onto a crumbling stone wall half a mile away?
SARAH	You could do worse than Terry O'Donohue's picture shows, and anyway you have to listen to them, the sound bounces round the village like a volley of machine gun fire. You might as well watch and get the pictures too.

Sean enters covered in oil.

SEAN	I should have taken that car down the back lane and shot it years ago.
SARAH	What's up with it now?
SEAN	Gear box, starter motor? Sure I don't know one end of the car from the other but the long and the short of it is that the blasted thing won't go.
SARAH	Do you want to borrow my bike?
SEAN	That old bone shaker? I wouldn't get to the top of the hill on that death machine. I'll get a lift from Dr Casey, I saw him down the way earlier. So I'll see you later. Do you want to come with me Brian? There's a bit of a fair in the town?
BRIAN	Alright.
SEAN	God bless then.
SARAH	See you later.

Sean and Brian exit.

SARAH	How are you feeling today?
MICHAEL	Fine.
SARAH	Really? You must have had a miracle worked on you then.

They exchange a look.

MICHAEL	My head's killing me, God, I don't know what I drank last night. (Pause) You were very nice.
SARAH	Ah now your memory's muddled up. I've never been nice in me life, I was just trying to be a responsible citizen.
MICHAEL	Really?
SARAH	Protecting property, I didn't want you falling over backwards and breaking the place to pieces.
MICHAEL	Oh I see.
SARAH	Thanks for writing back to me.
MICHAEL	I didn't have much choice.
SARAH	I know but there's no one else near enough to come.
MICHAEL	Except muggins here. Anyway he looks strong as a horse to me.
SARAH	Well he isn't. Oh I know the act well enough but that last heart attack nearly took him.
MICHAEL	It's only guilt brought me over. Guilt.
SARAH	Whatever brought you, I'm sure he's glad you came.
MICHAEL	He could always make you feel guilty, even after everything he's done, He could always make you feel like it was your fault.

They listen to the sea.

MICHAEL	I was a long time awake after you went last night.
SARAH	That's amazing, I thought you would have been out like a light.
MICHAEL	It was warm, wasn't it ? And I could smell the blossom coming up from the road, just like you said.
SARAH	Did you not want to go into the town today ?
MICHAEL	No.

SARAH   Why not ? You're missing the fair. What'll you
                     do with yourself ? Sit around the yard all day ?

MICHAEL   I might.

SARAH   (getting up) Right you are then.

MICHAEL   Are you going ?

SARAH   I can't spend the day in a daze, I have things to
                     do.

Michael opens a bottle.

                     Do you want a drink ?

SARAH   You drink too much.

MICHAEL   Who are you, me mother ?

Michael drinks.

SARAH   Do you want a game of tiddly winks ?

MICHAEL   Do you happen to have a set on you ?

SARAH   There's one inside.

Sarah exits for the tiddly winks. She re-enters and sets the game up
on the table.

Michael continues to look at her a little too closely.

SARAH   Red or blue ?

MICHAEL   You choose.

SARAH   Red, no cheating.

MICHAEL   You could smell it last night, the blossom,
                     couldn't you ? Couldn't you ?

SARAH   Play.

MICHAEL   Couldn't you ?

SARAH   Play.

They play a few turns of the game.

The night darkens, it is later. The sound of the sea.

SARAH   That's the first breath of air we've had all day.

Sarah leans back and closes her eyes. Michael watches her. She
pours herself a drink from his bottle.

SARAH   Being in the sunshine will do you good.

MICHAEL   It has vitamins, hasn't it ?

SARAH   It has. Good for your poor old skin.

Pause.

24

	You never talk about the accident.
MICHAEL	I've got one hell of a scar, it's just as well I don't make a living modelling swimming trunks.
SARAH	Just as well.
MICHAEL	I had to get a special card to let me through the security gates at the airport, I set the machines off. Small children with magnets stick to my leg like glue.
SARAH	Was it bad ?

Michael says nothing.

	It must have been bad. And leaving a job you've been in for so long, you come out feeling like you're a stranger to the world.
MICHAEL	I was. I didn't know anyone who wasn't in the Mob, the Navy. All my mates, you don't know civvies . . . maybe it's like leaving a convent.

Michael thinks for a moment.

MICHAEL	I can't . . . .I'm sorry, but I just can't see you being a nun, that's all.
SARAH	Takes all sorts. I wasn't young and I wasn't stupid.

Pause.

	They sent me to Africa, famine relief.
MICHAEL	Was it good, the famine work ? Did it feel good?
SARAH	You're a mystery Michael Foley, do you know that ? Of all the things I've been asked, I've never been asked if it was good. People say, 'that must have been terrible, all that misery, all that death'.
MICHAEL	That's just their own fear coming out though, isn't it ? That's just about them.
SARAH	I was a medical technician in Tanzania. Lack of medicine, lack of water, they were the killers, never lack of hope, isn't that strange ? If you had a wave of serious dehydration cases and no medicine, we used to get in the landrover and go looking for Coke. If you boil Coke and inject them with it, it gets their electrolight levels up. You see in a terrible crisis, when there's no medicine, no government support, no water, there's always Coke.

MICHAEL	What brought you back ?
SARAH	My mother had a stroke, they wouldn't give me enough time to be with her. That's a bit of a contradiction now, wouldn't you say ? I came home.

The sea comes and goes.

	I didn't know anything when I went out there.
MICHAEL	And what do you know now ?
SARAH	Life is precious, that's all I know. We should be glad.

Sean and Brian enter.

SEAN	Excuse us, excuse us, a bit of Free State Border if you please.
BRIAN	Free State Border ?
SEAN	A bit of order thank you for Brian Foley and his specially commended Lump of Grass !
BRIAN	It got a ribbon and everything and we only dug it up round the back of the church.
SARAH	Sean !
SEAN	I'm telling you Sarah, they were all lined up, self satisfied smug little donkeys so they were, pouring liquid fertilizer on their pots of grass all year, and up the judge comes to Brian's contribution, and he says 'Mrs Hennessey, I've never seen grass as comely as they in all me born days,' and Mrs Hennessey says to Brian, tell them Brian . . . .
BRIAN	'Do you mind young man if I smell your grass . . . '

Brian and Sean are in fits.

SEAN	. . . And I'm hoping to God no big fat bull is after doing his business on that bit of the back field, and her highness perusing its blades . . .
BRIAN	And I got 'Specially Commended' with a ribbon and a lucky horse shoe . . .
SEAN	So off with us to O'Toole's to congratulate ourselves with a celebratory jar, and the champion grass set up on the table in front of us for all and sundry to admire and wonder at.
SARAH	You'll be struck down.

BRIAN	And we saw the Headless Man. It was brilliant.
SARAH	You didn't go spending a pound on that nonsense ?
BRIAN	We went in twice.
SEAN	Do you remember the Headless Man Mike ?
MICHAEL	Mum wouldn't take us in.
SEAN	Didn't I take you in ?
MICHAEL	You used to go with the other men at night, you never went with us.
SEAN	Anyhow . . .

Sean picks up a bucket and plonks it on the head of a statue of the Virgin Mary.

SEAN	Ladies and gentlemen, he's a rocker he's a roller . . .
BRIAN	He's a mover he's a groover . . .
SEAN	A real live man without a head . . .
BRIAN	He's pick his nose . . .
SEAN	If he had nose to pick . . . sustained entirely by these green liquids sucked up from these jars at his feet . . .
BRIAN	He used to be an airline pilot, but he had no head for heights . . .
SEAN	The one and only in the whole of Ireland, put your hands together for . . .
SEAN/BRIAN	The Headless Man !

Sean and Brian present the statue to the others.

Scene Five

Later That Night.

Brian and Sean are setting up a table in the yard with a few chairs on top of it. They sit down on the chairs and crane their necks to se the film in the distance.

| SEAN | It's no good, I'm not in the right position. |
| SARAH | There, that's it, Sylvester Stallone! |

SEAN	Where ?
SARAH	There.
SEAN	Maybe I need glasses.
SARAH	Isn't it the limit that tonights the one night in the whole summer that it has to be windy.
SEAN	I can't hear a thing.
SARAH	Well you won't, that's what I'm after telling you, you won't til the wind changes.
BRIAN	Do you want to sit here grandad ?
SEAN	Go on then, give us a twist of your chair.

Brian and Sean swap seats.

SEAN	That's it ! I've got it ! I can see him now ! Four years we had the Sound of Music, and because of the wonky leg on the projector, I never got to see Julie Andrews' head once. We'd get a first rate view of her knees singing 'Climb Every Mountain'.

Sarah is getting a pot of tea ready. She comes and goes from the kitchen.

SARAH	It's lovely when she makes the children those clothes out of the curtains though, isn't it ?
SEAN	If anyone tried to run up a suit of clothes out of our curtains I don't know what they'd look like. They'd be rubbed red raw.

Michael stands in the yard watching. Sarah comes back out.

SARAH	Remember the old nun, she's probably dead now, she sang, 'how do you solve a problem like Maria'.
SEAN	Was it Margaret Rutherford ?
SARAH	(to Brian) What's he like ?
SEAN	I don't know who you're on about.
MICHAEL	I thought you'd know everything about that film, being a nun yourself.
SARAH	Oh that's right, they don't even consider you to be a nun in Ireland unless you can sing every song from The Sound of Music.
MICHAEL	Is that right ?
SARAH	And novices have to spend their time trying to

	look the spit of Audrey Hepburn in The Nun's Story.
SEAN	That was a great film. Wasn't that Katherine Hepburn ?

Michael is by the sea wall, looking out over he water.

Sarah joins him.

SARAH	You're missing the picture.

They both look out to sea.

SARAH	It's lovely looking at the boats at night, isn't it ? Imagining to yourself where they might be going. My mother used to say they all went to America. She had a sister who went to New York in the fifties, in those days when they went they never came back. 'Wave to the people on the emigrant boat' she'd say, and we'd wave and wave until our arms ached. I used to think it'd be wonderful to be on it, sailing away in the middle of the night to a new life, now I wouldn't be anywhere else in the world.
SEAN	Is that on the film or is the wall of the pub on fire ?
BRIAN	It's on the film.
MICHAEL	I used to think this was a lovely house.
SARAH	Have you noticed something Michael, you always put everything in the past tense. This still is a lovely house.
SEAN	What kind of a gun is that he has ?
MICHAEL	I was seventeen when I walked out of this town and joined up. Four years older than Brian.
SEAN	I've never seen a gun like that before in me life.
MICHAEL	Now listen to me, amn't I the lovely speaker ? I sound more English than the English themselves, no one would ever know.
SEAN	Have we eaten all the chocolate ?
SARAH	There's some diabetic chocolate.
SEAN	That stuff ! That's like eating an old slab of cardboard.

Pause.

What's up now, the film's stopped.

SARAH	It must have been hard for you in England.
MICHAEL	But I am hard. A hard man.
	What's keeping you out here in the back of beyond Sarah?
SARAH	What kind of question is that?

Pause. Michael won't let her get out of answering.

	It'll do for me. I have my mother's house next door, and the ocean in my front garden, and they're all as mad as hatters in the village so I'm in good company.

Pause.

	This is your home too Michael.
MICHAEL	No it's not. I've been away too long. You can't go back.

Michael exits for more drink.

SEAN	What's up now, the films stopped?
SARAH	It's ten to eleven, Terry's probably nipped into Nancy's for last orders.
SEAN	Leaving us on the edge of our seats like that, it's unscrupulous. Still, maybe it's just as well, I'm stiff as a board sitting up here on the table like a hat on the Eiffel Tower.

Sean gets down off the table.

SARAH	Mind yourself now.
SEAN	Ah go on out of that, I'm not dead yet.

Sean exits.

Brian has gone over to the sea wall, Sarah joins him.

SARAH	What are you up to?
BRIAN	Looking for seals.
SARAH	What do you think about all this Brian?
BRIAN	About what?
SARAH	Your dad and your grandad and all this goings on.
BRIAN	I think they're as bad as each other.

They look at the sea.

BRIAN	Have you got a boyfriend?

30

SARAH	Yes.
BRIAN	Have you?
SARAH	Why shouldn't I?
BRIAN	No reason. How come we never see him?
SARAH	That's a long story.
BRIAN	So you don't live together?
SARAH	What is this, market research?
BRIAN	Is that one a seal?
SARAH	No, it's only an old tyre.
BRIAN	Will you get married to him, your boyfriend?
SARAH	No. He's not the marrying kind.
BRIAN	I'm never getting married and having kids. People have kids just cause that's what everyone else does. That's not right is it? Why have them if you don't want them?
SARAH	You're an old soul Brian and no mistake.
BRIAN	What's that?
SARAH	It's something we say here. It means that you might be thirteen but inside you know things the rest of us can't see.

Sarah goes to Michael who continues drinking.

SARAH	Your dad's happy. He was in a terrible state last time. You know what he's like, won't let anyone do anything for him. He thinks the world of you, you know Michael.
MICHAEL	He makes me sick. Oh he's great at playing 'Grandad' now but you should have seen him the night I left home, standing in the kitchen, banging the table, saying, 'you need never come back, do you hear me? You need never come back and darken my door again'.
SARAH	Do you not think he's changed?
MICHAEL	He'll go to his grave thinking he's God's gift.

Sean enters carrying a hurley stick.

SEAN	I knew I still had it. I knew it.
SARAH	Have you been up that ladder, do I have to watch you every second? It's like being in charge of a crazed two year old.

BRIAN	What is it?

Michael examines the stick.

SEAN	It used to be Mike's.
BRIAN	Is it hockey or something?
SEAN	Hockey? Jesus Mary and Joseph.
SARAH	Your grandad's going to have a fit Brian.
SEAN	Hockey.
SARAH	That's a hurley stick Brian, or when women play the game it's called camogie, and it's a much better game I might add.
MICHAEL	Are you codding me?
SARAH	I'm explaining to Brian and I'm doing no more than giving him God's honest truth. You see Brian, when men play hurley it's all brute force and belting each other over the head with their sticks and poking each other in the eye and grunting and hammering at anything that gets in the way, whereas when we women play it's more like an art, all strategy and technique and tactics, and then we belt each other over the heads and beat anyone to death that gets in our way.
SEAN	It's a very traditional game Brian. Finn McCool used to play hurling with a pig's bladder.
SARAH	We don't do that anymore though Brian, we go to the shop and buy a little ball like this which is much more hygenic.

Michael gives the ball a knock.

MICHAEL	So you used to play then Sarah?
SEAN	She was captain of Carraroe All Girls under 14's.
MICHAEL	Carraroe! Those murderers!
SARAH	We were tough I'll grant you.
MICHAEL	Tough! You'd see the John's Ambulances lined up all the way to Dromore to take away the wounded and the dead.
SARAH	We were doing them a favour. Those first aiders were in desperate need of some patients to practise on.

Sean gets back up on the table.

SEAN	Yous can all sit in the cheap seats, I'm up in the balcony.

Sarah waters the flowers, Brian joins her.

BRIAN	Those ones look dead.
SARAH	They do right enough, but they're alright, these are the herbs.
MICHAEL	He used to plant carrot seeds in the window boxes at home.
BRIAN	Yeah it was a big joke, wasn't it?
MICHAEL	Sorry I spoke.
SARAH	Window boxes are great. You could grow any of these in a window box.
BRIAN	What's this one?
SARAH	That's Forget Me Not, the Egyptians used to put that on their eyelids to bring dreams.
MICHAEL	Not hayfever?
SARAH	And the Romans used to stick their wounds together with the juice of daffodil bulbs.
BRIAN	Did they?
SEAN	That was in the days before elastoplast was it?
SARAH	Oh you're a great pair of comedians aren't you?
SEAN	This bloody film won't be up again to midnight. I might go down the corner.
MICHAEL	"Down the Corner" is an Irish expression Brian, it means if I'm not mistaken, the public house.
BRIAN	I know what it means.
MICHAEL	Do you now, well that's a pity. I'd like you to grow up not knowing what any of this means. I'd like you to be a foreigner here, a nice English boy.
SEAN	What do you mean by that?
MICHAEL	What I said.
SEAN	That you don't want him to be Irish?
MICHAEL	What good has being Irish ever done me?
SARAH	Shush. It's a fox.

Everyone looks in the direction of the fox.

SEAN	The king of the fairies was turned into a fox and he had to wander the countryside for a hundred

33

	years until he found a woman who could love him for his heart and not for his power.
MICHAEL	(Looking at Sarah) And did he find a woman to care for him?
SEAN	No one knows. Maybe that's him now.
SARAH	Sean, you should be taking your injection now and not forgetting to eat.
SEAN	God, as if it wasn't bad enough I have to stab myself in the rear end with a needle every four hours.
SARAH	Ah go on and get it over with.
SEAN	She's like that old one in the pictures who is it? "She who must be obeyed".

Sean Exits.

SARAH	Look at that moon, it's like daylight out here.
SEAN(off)	I bet you don't get a moon like that in England.

Sarah goes to cross to the kitchen, Michael blocks her path.

MICHAEL	No da, there's no moon in England atall.

Michael moves aside, he drinks the end of his bottle and exits for another.

SARAH	We're funny here Brian, too full of stories and strangeness and do you know why? We've been with our backs to the sea for far too long.
SEAN	The English did that to us. Do you think they'll show the second half tonight Sarah?
BRAIN	I'm English.
SEAN	Sarah? Do you think Terry O'Donoghue's gone home or what? I'm not a mind reader.
SEAN (sings)	Oh all the money that ere I spent I spent in good company And all the harm that ere I done Alas it was to none but me And if it falls unto my lot That I should rise and you should not . . .

You're an immigrant child Brian, that's what you are.

Can you see Galway? Sometimes you can see Galway From up there when it's a fine night. |

Michael enters still drinking.

MICHAEL   I went up into the cupboard to see if I could find
                 Berni's hurley stick. It's piled high with Sarah's
                 clothes. How long have you two been living
                 together?

End of Act One.

ACT TWO

Scene Six

The next day.

Sean sits in the yard carving a commemorative stone.

Brian is watering the flowers. Sarah is seated reading the newspaper.

We hear a full band version of the song played earlier on the radio, County Leitrim Queen.

> For centuries in Leitrim soil her great ancestors
> dwelt
> Til one who married into them
> Usurped the land they held
> I saw the rose fade from her cheeks
> Her birthright loss was keen
> She pined, she died
> My joy, my pride
> God rest my little Leitrim Queen.

SARAH	Shout out now when I get to a horse you like the sound of. Are you right?
SEAN/BRIAN	Yeah.
SARAH	Kilbeggin this is. Kamtara, Nordic Beat, Genesta, Kilkilcastle . . .
SEAN	Kil what?
SARAH	Kilkilcastle.
SEAN	That's a stupid name, sure no one could say that.
SARAH	Michael's Star . . . listen, there's one called Michael's Star. We should back that for Michael. Go inside Brian and see what's in the money box beside the Sacred Heart picture in the kitchen.
BRIAN	Which picture is it?
SARAH	You'd think we were the National Gallery inside. The one with Jesus with his heart showing.
SEAN	With sticky out hands.
SARAH	Sean!

36

Brian exits.

SARAH	He's enjoying himself now.
SEAN	It's well for him
SARAH	Will you not go down the road and talk to Michael?
SEAN	I can't talk to him, can't you get that through your skull? There's no talking to him about anything. If he wants to talk I'll listen, I can't say fairer than that.
SARAH	You're like two horses yoked together and pulling in opposite directions choking each other. You'd rather strangle each other than work together for two minutes. Is it so hard for you to tell the boy you love him?
SEAN	Sure, I'm no good at that kind of mularky.

Brian enters

BRIAN	Two pounds 38 pence.
SARAH	That's grand. We can flither away our last few pence on the horses now.
SEAN	You'll be struck down.
SARAH	Do you want to go down the corner Brian and see if your dad's alright?
BRIAN	No. I'm glad when he goes down the pub. I'm glad when he's not here.

Sarah goes to Sean and looks over his shoulder as he works. She kisses him familiarly on the cheek. Michael enters and sees this.

SARAH (to Michael)
I'm just off down the bookies to spend our last two pounds. There's a horse called Michael's Star. Will I put a few bob on it for you?

MICHAEL	Why not.
SARAH	I'm off then
BRIAN	Can I come too?
SARAH	Come for the walk.

Sarah and Brian exit.

Sean and Michael sit at the table in silence.

MICHAEL	I'm going to book our tickets back to England.
SEAN	Right you are.

MICHAEL	I wouldn't want to get in your way. I'm sure you and Sarah want to be on your own.
SEAN	This is my house, do you hear me?
MICHAEL	When has it ever been anything else but your house, never anyone else's, never Mam's.

Brian appears on the sea wall.

BRIAN	We forgot the money.

Brian collects the money off the table but he doesn't go.

MICHAEL	Will you get married or just shack up together?
SEAN	I'll swing for you, you little skite.
MICHAEL	This is the man who kicked my sister out because he found her snogging in the yard with a punk rocker.
SEAN	I did not kick her out.
MICHAEL	You might as well have done, and she never came back.
SEAN	Is that my fault? I did everything a father could do, I slaved for the lot of yous.

Sarah enters.

MICHAEL	Here we go.
SEAN	And what thanks did I get for it?
MICHAEL	You did what you wanted. The whole family circulated around him and he still didn't have a good word to say for any of us. We ran, ran from him, we couldn't get away fast enough.
SEAN (to Sarah)	This is the fella you wanted me to ask over.
MICHAEL	Sure you've never handed out an invitation in your life.
SEAN	And you never took one. How often did your mother ask you to come home?
MICHAEL	It suited you down to the ground to get Mam to do your dirty work for you.
SEAN	You drove your mother into her grave.
MICHAEL	I did! Jesus Christ! Jesus!
SEAN	"The children. The children" I had the ears worn off me with her bleating on day and night, night and day about the children, but Mr Bloody Gone To England here wouldn't shift his arse and

deign to pay her a visit so precious was his time.
You broke your mother's heart.

Michael swings round and hits the side of the house with his crutch.

MICHAEL	Oh you'd know all about the breaking of hearts. D'you see, I'm the villain, never him, he's totally innocent.
SEAN	And Mr Big here couldn't be arsed, couldn't be arsed.
MICHEAL	You broke her heart a long time before I ever did.
SEAN	What do you know? He thinks he knows how the world turns and him not even born when me and his mum were in our heyday.
MICHAEL	Heyday! He killed her, destroyed her with promises that never came true.
SEAN	I worked me back off all those years, I suppose that counts for nothing at all?
MICHAEL	She had one coat, do you know that, one coat all my childhood through, winter and summer.
SEAN	Sure I'd have bought her a coat but you know what she was like.
MICHAEL	Did you! Jesus! Did you know what she was like?
SEAN	Wasn't she my wife?
MICHAEL	You were never her husband.
SEAN	Where was I? Where was I then, tell me? Was it off with other women you thought I was? Do you know Sarah, I worked in Coventry once for five shillings an hour, and I went without, I went without God knows what, he'll never have the rights of it.
MICHAEL	Him, going without? You never went without your pint. You never went without your Sunday dinner, with mam giving you meat off her plate.
SEAN	What are you saying? You're demented.
MICHAEL	I'm saying she gave you her own food and you never said no. "Your mother eats like a doormouse".
SEAN	What are you on about now, I can't understand a word of it.

MICHAEL	You won't even admit it now, will you? You'd die rather then say you were ever in the wrong.
SEAN	One more spit out of you mister and I'll give you such a dunt you won't know yourself.
MICHAEL	Come near me and I'll kill you.
SEAN	What'll you do, give me a poke with your crutch?
MICHAEL	I wish I'd beaten the tar out of you once before I had my accident.
SEAN	You! You could never have hit me. Give him a jab in the ribs and he'd have been sitting on his mothers lap balling.
SARAH	Jesus Christ! Jesus, will you both shut up.
SEAN	Stay out of this Sarah, this is between the boy and me.
MICHAEL	The boy! The boy!
SARAH	And I'm meant to stay out?
SEAN	It's family business, private.
SARAH	Am I not family so?
MICHAEL	Oh God Sarah you don't want to be part of this family, unless you're born into it and have no escape.
SEAN	I told you to watch your mouth.
MICHAEL	I'm only telling Sarah the truth. Tell us Sarah, does he shag you? Does he? He used to do it to mam when she didn't want to.

Sean wails through his gritted teeth.

	Isn't that right da? She used to get me to say I was sick so she could sleep in my bed and he'd leave her alone.
SEAN	You dirty bastard.
MICHAEL	I'm only saying what happened, I was only a child, I wasn't even Brian's age.
SEAN	I can't stand it, I can't stand you.
MICHAEL	You forced everyone, didn't you, not only mam, you forced us all, ground us down, bent us to your will, is it any wonder we left?

Sean lunges at Michael, at the last moment he falls upon his half

finished stonework and starts to beat the statues and granite slabs
with a mallet. He kicks the tin boxes of chisels and steel rules, and
flings everything around in a tantrum of rage and frustration. Sarah,
Michael and Brian watch, half astounded, half afraid for their own
safety.

Finally Sean's rage subsides. He stops amidst the confusion and
gets his breath back.

SEAN   Every family has its ups and downs isn't that
                right?

Pause.

                That's what I think anyway.

Michael exits to the kitchen.

BRIAN   I wish he was dead. I wish he'd been killed in
                the accident. He ruins everything.

SEAN   Shut your mouth you. I never want to hear that
                kind of talk out of you again, do you hear me?
                Do you?

BRIAN   Yes.

Brian exits over the wall.

SARAH   (Calling after him) Brian! Brian!

Sarah turns to look at Sean. He doesn't return her gaze.

SARAH   You're determined so?

SEAN   What are you going on about now? Isn't it your
                man who started it? What did I do? Tell me? I've
                been killing meself over his lordship inside and
                what do I get back for it, will you answer me
                that? Filthy talk and a sneer in his eye. Oh I see
                it . . . . Does he think I don't see it?

SARAH   I despair of you Sean.

Sarah exits. Sean starts to put the yard to rights, then he sits down
halfheartedly, amidst the debris.

Brian enters over the sea wall with seaweed and shells.

The sound of the sea comes and goes.

SEAN   I'm after belting the Virgin Mary over the head
                with a hammer, will you look? She's got a chip
                gone out of her forehead now. That's me packing
                me bags for hell and no mistake.

The sea washes up to the shore.

	What colour is the sea tonight?
BRIAN	Grey.
SEAN	It's grey is it? And is it noisey?
BRIAN	Just the waves.
SEAN	That'll be the water breaking on the black stone of the islands. Do you like that noise?
BRIAN	Yes there was a fox on the beach.
SEAN	Was it the poor old king of the fairies?
BRIAN	Yes, I knew it was him.

Sean makes a move to go inside. On his way over to the kitchen door he tidies up a bit. Pulling a cloth off one of the stoneworks, he discovers a stone owl, small and neatly carved. Sean looks at it astonished.

SEAN	What's this? God bless us and save us. Will you look at the lovely feathers on him, and his little beak and all.
BRIAN	It's an owl.
SEAN	I can see that. I can see that. When did your dad do it Brian? Did you see him at it?
BRIAN	He didn't do it, I did.
SEAN	You did?
BRIAN	It's too small. If you make a mistake you have to keep making it smaller. Can I go back down to the water one more time before bed?
SEAN	Go on with you then.

Brian exits. Sean is left staring at the owl. Michael enters.

SEAN	Your boy made this.
MICHAEL	Did he now. I suppose you'd like him to kill himself and be a stone mason.
SEAN	You have an artist for a child. To be able to make something beautiful is a gift from God. I never had it.

Sean exits. Michael is left looking at the owl. Brian appears on the sea wall with shells and seaweed.

Pause.

MICHAEL	We're going back.
BRIAN	When?

MICHAEL	As soon as I can book the tickets. What's the sulky face for?
BRIAN	Does Grandad know?
MICHAEL	Yes 'Grandad' knows. If they think I'm hanging around here playing happy families they have another think coming.
BRIAN	Maybe you won't be able to get tickets.
MICHAEL	What's up with you now?
BRIAN	I don't want to go back yet.
MICHAEL	What?
BRIAN	I don't want to go back. Why couldn't we stay for a bit longer?
MICHAEL	I don't believe I'm hearing this. You were the one who kicked up the big fuss about coming over at all. Why? Why do you want to stay on?
BRIAN	I like it here.
MICHAEL	Fine. Fine. You like it here, then you can stay. I'll go back on my own. I couldn't care less what you do.

Sarah enters over the wall from the beach.

SARAH	Has he stormed off in a huff?

Michael doesn't reply.

	He usually storms off in a huff and then I have to go after him and get him to talk.
MICHAEL	You're just like a proper married couple then, aren't you?
SARAH	Is that how it was with your wife?
MICHAEL	Don't . . . don't bring my wife into this.
SARAH	Maybe I should never have asked you over, it's just, Michael, he talks about you. He does care about you.

Michael remains silent.

	I know you two have had a difficult time, but honest to God, you should have heard him telling me about when you were a child. He feels like he's lost everything.
MICHAEL	The poor bastard. The poor lonely old bastard. Do you want me to feel sorry for him now, is that it?

SARAH	I just don't want you to realise too late . . . to have missed the chance to have talked, believe me Michael, you'll always regret it.
MICHAEL	Jesus ! Jesus Christ ! You don't know anything about what happened between us. The years he had, the years and years he had, to speak, to say anything, to make one single gesture. And if he's a pathetic old man now, well I'm sorry for him, in the same way I'd feel sorry for any bitter selfish old bastard. I couldn't give a toss what he's said to you when he's crying into his pint pot. He's always cornered the market in self pity. You should have heard him, there's nothing that's gone wrong in his life that isn't someone else's fault. And you know Sarah, I wonder why you think you're so well qualified to advise me on my personal life ? What makes you so superior to the rest of us ? It seems to me that you spend so much of your time trying to save us all from ourselves, you haven't got much left for living your own life atall. I mean, first you lock yourself up in a convent, can't get more out of this world than that, can you ? Then you team up with an old codger on his last legs, not much risk involved there, is there ?
SARAH	I'm not going to listen to you if you're going to be like this.
MICHAEL	You fancied me when you first met me, didn't you ? Didn't you ?

Now, my guess is that your set life with father of the year upstairs leaves something to be desired, what would you say ? But you won't have much time for thinking about your own problems will you, not when you have to fill in telling the rest of us how to save ourselves and mend our ways. |
| SARAH | I never meant to do that. |
| MICHAEL | Go on like this Sarah and one day you'll wake up, and you'll be old. That's what happened to my mother. You're the same age I am Sarah, we're not young any more. I'd say you were past it in terms of having a baby. Soon you'll be alone, you see, we're not so different after all. Soon you'll be alone, just like me, only you'll be barren. |

Sarah looks at Michael. She is speechless, devastated.

44

Michael sees with horror that his words have found their target.

Sarah, shattered, leaves over the wall.

Michael stands in the yard, alone.

Scene Seven

Morning, the next day.

Brian is watering the herbs in the yard. The cases are packed.
Michael comes out and puts the jam on the table. He looks Brian,
but he doesn't speak. Michael goes back inside.

As soon as his father is gone, Brian gets up on the sea wall, and
collects his various bits of rope, shells and seaweed.

Sarah climbs up over the wall and empties the sand out of her
shoes.

SARAH   How ya Brian ?

BRAIN   Hello.

SARAH   Look, a prize shell.

She presents him with a piece of stone.

BRIAN   It's like a fossil, isn't it ?

SARAH   It's probably a bit of some old Irish dinosaur.

Sarah looks at the cases.

SARAH   So you're all packed then and ready for the
               plane?

BRIAN   Yeah.

Michael comes out and puts a knife on the table. He sees Sarah but
doesn't speak. He goes back inside the house.

SARAH   And where's your grandfather at this hour of the
               day ?

BRIAN   Don't know.

SARAH   Will you drop me a line and tell me how you're
               getting on ?

BRIAN   Yeah.

Pause.

45

Sarah, do you think it would be alright to say I come from here ? Or do I come from England ?

SARAH   You're allowed to choose Brian.

BRIAN   Am I ?

SARAH   Of course you are.

Brian sits on the wall, the sea comes and goes. Michael comes out and sits down at the table eating a piece of toast. For a moment no one speaks.

SARAH   Do you still have those window boxes at home Brian ?

BRIAN   Yeah, somewhere.

Sarah exits and comes back with some newspaper. She goes to the herbs.

SARAH   You can take some of the herbs back with you to grow over in England, would you like that ?

BRIAN   Won't they die ?

SARAH   Ah no, not if we wrap the roots up in newspaper, and wet it. We can put them in a plastic carrier.

Michael watches the woman and the boy working away together.

SARAH   Which ones do you like ?

BRIAN   You choose.

SARAH   Ahhhh no, they're for you, you choose now.

BRIAN   Any one ?

SARAH   Any one.

Brian chooses. Sarah carefully digs up the plants.

SARAH   Now, wrap them up, is that tight ? Dip it in the watering can, that's grand. Now when you get up in the morning and see your herbs, you'll think of us over here in this old bit of a garden.

SEAN   (off) Sarah ! Sarah !

SARAH   What is it ? Is he still in his bed ?

SEAN   Sarah !

Sarah goes inside.

Michael and Brian sit in silence. Michael gets on with having his breakfast.

Sarah comes out.

SARAH	Brian, will you go down to the village and give Dr.Casey a ring. Your grandfather's not feeling very well at all.

Scene Eight

Later Afternoon, the same day.

A campbed has been set up in the yard, and Sean is asleep in it, propped up by pillows.

Sarah and Michael sit at the table. Brian is moving shells around the table top.

MICHAEL	Shouldn't he be up in his bed ?
SARAH	He should, but that way he'd think he was on his last legs.
BRIAN	Is he ?
SARAH	He nearly died three months ago.
BRIAN	You should have told me.
MICHAEL	Should I now ? We could get a cab and take him to the hospital.
SARAH	He doesn't want to be in the hospital. He wants to be here.
MICHAEL	What did the doctor say ?
SARAH	Sometime in the next twenty-four hours.
MICHAEL	You're very cool, aren't you ?
SARAH	How do you expect me to be ?
BRIAN	Is he asleep ?
SARAH	It's a deep sleep Brian, I think he's probably slipping in and out of a coma by now.
MICHAEL	Christ this is all we need.

Sarah exits and comes back with a tumbler of water and a tweezers. She feels Sean's head.

SARAH	You're very hot, aren't you ? This is how to give him a drink Brian. He can't swallow so you have to help him, do you think you can do that ?
BRIAN	Yeah.

SARAH   You just dip this gauze in the water and then put
                   it on his lips like this. There.

Sarah gives the tweezers to Brian, Michael watches at a distance.

MICHAEL   This is crazy keeping him here. They can treat
                   him properly in hospital.

SARAH   Michael, they can't do anything for him in
                   hospital that we can't do here.

MICHAEL   It doesn't seem right to me.

SARAH   It's what he would have wanted.

MICHAEL   Oh yeah, and he always gets what he wants,
                   doesn't he ?

Sarah exits into the house.

Brian has gone over to the sea wall.

BRIAN   What will it look like ?

MICHAEL   What will what look like ?

BRIAN   When he dies. Will it be like a fit or something ?

MICHAEL   Brian ! I don't know. How do you expect me to
                   know a thing like that ?

BRIAN   It's alright, I'll ask Sarah.

MICHAEL   Fine. I'm sure she'll be able too give you all the
                   details.

Pause.

                   Oh she thinks she knows it all alight. Look at
                   him, still managing to to be the centre of
                   attention after all these years, it's amazing, isn't
                   it ? He never gave a toss about any of us, not a
                   toss. You know I think there were years when he
                   never really spoke, actually spoke to any of us at
                   all. He was never there. He wouldn't listen. You
                   couldn't even make him listen, he just shouted
                   you down, made you shut up by pure physical
                   force. I don't know why he ever had kids.

BRIAN   I don't know why you ever had kids.

MICHAEL   What ?

BRIAN   Nothing.

MICHAEL   What they hell is that meant to mean ?

BRIAN   Nothing.

MICHAEL   I want to hear. No you said something and I want
                   to know what you meant.

BRIAN	You're only here now because of the accident.
MICHAEL	So ? Come on, let's hear the rest.
BRIAN	All while mum was leaving you were never there.
MICHAEL	Oh I see, I'm the villain again. I was working Brian, I was in the Navy, we go away on ships, remember ?
BRIAN	You could have got leave.
MICHAEL	Oh could I ? You have it all worked out, don't you ?
BRIAN	I liked grandad.
MICHAEL	Jesus Christ ! You don't know what he did. You weren't there. That selfish bastard never thought about anyone but himself in his whole life.
BRIAN	Can't you just forget about what happened before ?
MICHAEL	No. I can't I can't.
BRIAN	All the things you go on about, all the things grandad did, you do them. You do all of them.

Brian goes back over to Sean, Michael is left alone.

Sarah sits down beside Sean, the newspaper in her hand. Michael lingers in the kitchen doorway, watching. He gets himself another bottle of Guinness.

SARAH	(to Sean) What will we have a few bob on ? Shout out now when you hear a name you like the sound of. Bray Boy, Kilmarnock, Follow On . . .

Michael brings a lamp over to Sarah.

MICHAEL	He looks different.
SARAH	His muscles are relaxing. But he's a terrible colour. Would you talk to him ?
MICHAEL	I wouldn't be able to think of anything to say.

Pause.

	Come on and take a break.
SARAH	I'm alright
MICHAEL	Even so.
BRIAN	Don't leave me on my own with him.

SARAH   There's nothing to be frightened of Brian, we'll
                 be just over here.

Sarah and Michael lean on the sea wall. The sound of the waves as
they come and go.

Ships' hooters call off the water.

SARAH   There's the ferry now.

MICHAEL   I suppose you've seen a lot of death.

SARAH   I suppose I have.

MICHAEL   It seems like the people who really want things
                 never get them, and the people who don't care
                 one way or another, it just falls right into their
                 laps.

They look out to sea.

                 I can't believe he's ended up with a lovely
                 woman like you.

SARAH   Don't think we haven't had our problems.

MICHAEL   But you stayed with him. I can't get over it.

Pause.

                 I used to sit up here on this wall when I was a
                 child and cry. He didn't allow us to cry so you
                 had to go and hide to do it. And tonight Brian
                 said that I'm just like him. What do you think
                 Sarah? Am I just like him? Like da?

SARAH   There's an old picture of Sean in one of the
                 drawers in the kitchen dresser inside. I'll show it
                 to you. He was nineteen when it was taken.
                 Smiling, leaning up against a van up by some
                 quarry in Carlow. Covered from head to toe in
                 the white dust from the stone. And then you
                 came, and it was like he'd walked straight out of
                 that picture, and he was young again. That's how
                 alike you are.

MICHAEL   Is this how it happens? You think you've done
                 everything for the best, and then you find that
                 everyone you love can't stand you for it?

SARAH   I don't know how it happens.

MICHAEL   I've messed it up with Brian. I have, haven't I?

SARAH   There's very little in life that can't be put right
                 with a few loving words.

MICHAEL   I'm no good at that kind of mullarky.

SARAH	Become good then, practise. Brian's good at it. Who was it went to you in the hospital and put honey on your muesli because he knew you didn't like the taste? If that isn't love, I don't know what is.

The night darkens.

Sarah puts oil on Sean's forehead, lips, hands and feet. It is part of the process of the last rites but she says no prayers.

Music, as time passes.

SARAH	Look, there's the first star out now. Why don't you read to him Brian, being read to is always lovely.
BRIAN	Can he hear me?
SARAH	I don't know love. They say the hearing is the last sense to go. There's a few books in the kitchen.

Brian exits to the kitchen. Sarah goes to Michael who is at the table. She takes the stout from his hand and drinks it. Brian comes back with the book and sits down beside Sean and reads to him.

BRIAN	(reads) A resident magistracy in Ireland is not an easy thing to come by nowadays, neither is it a very attractive job, yet on the evening when I first propounded the idea to the young lady who had recently consented . . .
SARAH	(to Michael) Brian's great isn't he? Will you give me a hand to turn him? He'll get sore.
MICHAEL	I can't.
SARAH	What is it, are you trying to get your own back on him?
MICHAEL	I just can't that's all.
SARAH	Well, if you can't, you can't.

Sarah goes back to Sean and she quietly shows Brian how to help her turn the sleeping man.

Later.

Michael refills the paraffin lamps. It is the cold chill before dawn.

MICHAEL	Will you not take him in now?
SARAH	No, I will not.
MICHAEL	It's nearly daylight.
SARAH	You'd love for it to be all out of your sight,

wouldn't you? Well that's too bad. I'm leaving
him in peace here. He's not budging.

Brian is dozing under a coat.

MICHAEL   Brian? Brian? Do you want to go up to bed?

BRIAN   No. I want to stay here.

Michael goes back to the sea wall. Sarah notices a change in Sean.

SARAH   You're getting very cold, aren't you?

BRIAN   Will I get another blanket?

Sarah looks at Michael but he will not meet her eyes.

SARAH   (to Sean) You're alright love, you're alright.
                  Brian, get a candle and some matches from the
                  kitchen.

Brian exits to the kitchen. Sarah sits stroking Sean's head. Brian
brings the candle back. Sarah lights the candle, and places it into
Sean's hands, she holds it there while stroking his head with her
other hand. Sean's breathing labours on, in the same pattern we
have become used to over the last while, yet it seems shallower
now. Michael can hear it too, although he shows no reaction. Sarah
holds the candle firmly for Sean, his breathing a little shallower
now, Sarah stroking his head all the time. Brian stands by the
bedside, and now, awkwardly, shyly, strokes his grandfather's
other hand, just once.

SARAH   We'll give him a candle to light his way into a
                  better place, isn't that right? A better place than
                  this one.

Sean is silent. We have hardly noticed the transition. The sea
rumbles up to the shore.

SARAH   There you are now, that's the best way to go. If I
                  don't die like that Sean Foley, I'll have a terrible
                  row with you when I see you next.

BRIAN   Is that all that happens?

SARAH   That's all that happens. They just stop breathing.

Michael has never moved.

Scene Nine

Morning.

Music.

The lamps are cleared away.

The body is laid out on the table, covered with a blanket. Sarah is drinking a bottle of stout, probably the only thing she could find in the house. She is washing the body, then carefully wiping it with a flannel and drying it with a towel.

Brian comes in with a clean shirt and socks.

SARAH   Good man Brian.

Brian stands watching.

               We want him to be presentable, don't we.

Sarah washes and wipes Seans hands.

               His poor hands. Look at those fingers, aren't
               they like sausages, aren't they? Thick, with the
               dirt ground into the flesh from all those years of
               work and the new skin grown over it.

Pause. Sarah continues washing the body.

Michael is sitting on the sea wall reading a letter.

SARAH   Can you wash his feet Brian?

BRIAN   Yeah.

Sarah goes over to the sea wall. She has the clean shirt still in her hands.

MICHAEL   He's given me the house. Why me?

SARAH   He knew you loved the house.

MICHAEL   Did he?

SARAH   This holiday's been a disaster.

MICHAEL   You wouldn't want to break family tradition
               would you, we've never had a holiday that hasn't
               been a disaster.

Sarah drinks.

SARAH   I have to get him dressed.

MICHAEL   I thought the undertakers would do that.

SARAH   No. It's us. There's a new shirt but it's all hard,
               scratchy. I suppose it doesn't matter now, but
               it feels like it does. He used to wear this one all
               the time.

53

Pause.

Sarah is overcome. Michael sits, unsure, lost.

> Will you put it on him for me?

Michael looks at Sarah.

> Will you put it on him for me? I need your help
> Michael. I can't do any more on my own.

Sarah offers Michael the shirt, after a moment he takes it. Michael goes to the body and watches Brian as he finishes drying Sean's feet. Brian goes and sits on the sea wall with Sarah. Michael, hopelessly lost, tries to get his father's arm in the shirt sleeve, eventually the only way he can do this is to hold Sean in his arms, half in and half out of the shirt.

He begins to sing;

MICHAEL Oh of all the money that ere I spent
      I spent it in good company
      And all the harm that ere I've done
      Alas it was to none but me
      And all I've done for want of wit
      To memory now I can't recall
      So fill to me the parting glass
      Goodnight and joy be with you all

Michael sits on the table holding his father and his tears start to come.

Brian watches.

> And if it falls unto my lot
> That I should rise and you should not
> I'll gently rise and softly call
> Goodnight and joy be with you all.

Sarah has been watching.

MICHAEL He used to sing that.

SARAH   I know.

MICHAEL He was never this clean when he was alive.

Music.

A pair of hands dumps a crate up on the wall. Michael watches after the person who must have left it as he retreats down the beach. Sarah joins him.

SARAH   See you Deccy, See you, thanks very much.

MICHAEL He's still wearing that cycling hat.

SARAH   Look at that, the dote, he's brought us something

for the wake and he hasn't two pennies to rub
together.

BRIAN   What's a wake?

Sarah is investigating the box.

MICHAEL   You're in Ireland now Brian, we'd never miss an
                opportunity for a party.

SARAH   Biscuits, bacon, tea, . . .

MICHAEL   Stout . . .

SARAH   Alkaseltzer!

MICHAEL   There's an experienced mourner if ever I saw
                one.

Michael and Sarah exchange a smile.

BRIAN   What do we do?

MICHAEL   We have a party to send the soul off on its
                journey.

BRIAN   There aren't enough of us for a party.

MICHAEL   We're not a crowd, it's true. But we have all the
                equipment, drink, music, rashers,

SARAH   And cake.

MICHAEL   And cake.

BRIAN   And cake?

MICHAEL   Jesus Brian, you can't achieve anything in
                Ireland without cake.

SARAH   Never a truer word spoken. Will we give the
                radio a belt and see if you can get a blast of
                music out of it.

No one is very sure what they should do next.

                Do you think Sean would want us sitting around
                in the dark like a bunch of goules? He would not.

Sarah makes a move towards the radio.

BRIAN   Can I do it?

SARAH   I wouldn't know if you could Brian, it takes
                years of practice to make that radio work.

Brian hits the radio, it comes on.

SARAH   Show off.

They stand around the body listening to the music.

MICHAEL	Look at us, we're like all those fellas in Frankenstein's Monster . . .
SARAH	That scene where they're waiting for the flash of lightning . . .
MICHAEL	All gathered round the body . . .
SARAH	Who was the one with the funny back . . .
MICHAEL	That wasn't Frankenstein . . .
SARAH	It was, he kept saying, master you promised to fix my back . . .
MICHAEL	That's the Hunchback of Notre Dame, that was Peter Laurie.
SARAH	He wasn't in Frankenstein . . .

Pause.

	If your dad was here, he'd say it was Michael Redgrave. He always said Michael Redgrave when he didn't have a clue.
MICHAEL	What do you mean, 'if he was here'. He is here.
SARAH	Yeah.
MICHAEL	Come on and we'll get this bottle open.

Michael opens the bottle and pours *four* glasses.

BRIAN	Who's this one for?
MICHAEL	For da.
SARAH	Sean would scalp us if we left him out.
BRIAN	Do you think he'd like that owl I made for his grave?
SARAH	Brian, he'd be made up. He loved that owl.

Michael swivels around and drinks Sean's glass down in one go. He turns to face the others innocently.

MICHAEL	God it must be a very dry journey to heaven, the corpse is after swigging down that drink in one gulp.
SARAH	He better have another then.
MICHAEL	I think he had.

Sarah pours Sean another drink.

The shipping forecast comes on the radio. Sarah belts it again and a wild reel bursts out of the machine.

Sarah grabs Brian and whisks him around in a dance. Michael watches while alternately pouring himself and his father drinks. The dance ends.

MICHAEL   Will you give us a toast Sarah?

SARAH   To Sean.

ALL   To Sean.

SARAH   That's the send off he would have loved. Go on now and get some rest.

MICHAEL   Will you be alright?

SARAH   I'll be grand.

Michael and Brian exit.

Sarah waters the flowers and spends a little time taking in everything in the yard. The sea comes and goes.

She picks the blossom from one of the plants and she places it on Seans eyes.

SARAH   To bring you dreams.

Sarah sits down beside the body.

Scene Ten

Morning, three days later.

The yard is flooded with sunshine and everything is put back to rights. Michael comes out of the kitchen leaning only on a walking stick now.

Sarah is watering the flowers.

The sound of the sea.

Michael watches her for a few moments.

MICHAEL   So . . . we're finally off.

SARAH   The place'll seem empty now without you both.

MICHAEL   You should live in this house Sarah, it was meant to be lived in, it's your home as much as anyone else's.

Pause.

               I can't believe I said those things.

SARAH   All over and done now.

MICHAEL	You were good to us, me and dad.
SARAH	Have you checked your two rooms now, ah well if you've forgotten anything I can always send it on except the postage is a sin, I don't know how they have the nerve to ask the money they ask. It'd be cheaper to put it under your arm and take it on the plane yourself.
MICHAEL	I didn't mean it. It was me I was talking about, it was me, not you.
SARAH	Ah who's to say you didn't have the rights of it.

She looks out to sea.

SARAH	They say the weather will break tomorrow. Then we'll be plunged into winter before you know it.

Pause.

	What'll we do with all this stone.
MICHAEL	Leave it where it is. I wouldn't know this place if it was organised.

Brian comes into the yard eating his cornflakes.

	Are you not ready yet?
BRIAN	What?
MICHAEL	If you're not careful, you'll make us miss the plane.
BRIAN	I will? What about you in the bath for an hour?

Sarah goes into the kitchen with the watering can.

BRIAN	You were born into this house on a fine summering day like this one, in the big bedroom upstairs.
MICHAEL	Who told you that?
BRIAN	Grandad. And after he took Berni up to see you, she made him come outside and put bread on the wall for the stork.
MICHAEL	I never knew that. Will we go down to the sea one last time before we go?
BRIAN	We haven't got time.
MICHAEL	Come on Brian.

Michael struggles onto the sea wall. Brian follows him.

They climb up and as they do, the yard is transformed into the sea.

Waves crash and ebb.

The boy and the man listen to the sea.

MICHAEL   The Atlantic isn't like any other ocean in the
            world. I don't know why it feels different, but it
            does.

            We could get in, couldn't we?

BRIAN   Get into the sea?

MICHAEL   It's lovely and warm. We could just get in, in our
            shorts.

Pause.

            Come on Brian.

Michael lets his stick fall to the sand and lets Brian support him.

He struggles to take his shoes off.

MICHAEL   Come on, what are you waiting for?

BRIAN   Dad, I'm scared of the water.

MICHAEL   It's alright Brian, I'll do a deal with you. You
            don't let me fall over and I won't let you drown.

Slowly Brian takes off his shoes.

Music starts to rise and blend with the sound of the waves.

Brian and Michael walk forward into the water, supporting each
other.

Sean appears on the sea wall and watches them.

The End.

An Instant Playscript

Waking first published in Great Britain in 1997
as a paperback original by Nick Hern Books Limited,
14 Larden Road, London W3 7ST
in association with the Soho Theatre Company, London

Typeset by Country Setting, Woodchurch, Kent, TN26 3TB
Printed and bound in Great Britain

ISBN 1 85459 392 7

A CIP catalogue record for this book is available from
the British Library

WAKING

Lin Coghlan

When Michael reluctantly returns
to Ireland with his young son, it's
not long before old wounds are
opened up between him and his
own father. If it were not for Sarah,
who lives next door, the visit would
be short lived, but now, during a
relentless heatwave on the edge
of the Atlantic coast, Michael starts
to open up to the strange young
woman . . .

Premiered by the Soho Theatre
Company as the first production
in their new home in the heart of
London, Lin Coghlan's lyrical new
play offers a tender portrait of
three generations of men, circling
each other but never succeeding
in getting truly close.

Lin Coghlan has been writing
for ten years, mainly for young
peoples' theatre. *Waking* resulted
from her association with the Soho
Theatre Company, for which she
was Writer in Residence in 1995.

PLAYS **£6.50**

ISBN 1-85459-392-7

9 781854 593924

Published in conjunction with the
Soho Theatre Company, this 'Instant
Playscript' is intended to reflect the
immediacy of the play on the stage.
It is printed direct from the author's
own disk prepared only a few days
before opening night. The aim is to
give audiences at the theatre and
readers all over the world instant
access to the best of current new
writing as it hits the stage.